AF261446

THE BOY AND THE BAGEL NECKLACE

by Lisa Soland

Illustrated by

Sanghamitra Dasgupta

This book is lovingly dedicated

to our friend, Stephen.

The Boy and the Bagel Necklace

Chapter 1

The Orphanage

Hi. My name is Andrew, and I'm seven years old. I know what you're thinking. I'm short for my age. But that's what happens when you're young, and you don't get enough to eat. I grew up in an orphanage that had too many children.

It's not that my parents didn't want me. Don't think that because that will get you nowhere. My birth parents were poor, but they were smart. They knew they would make bad parents, and you have to be smart to come up with that idea.

We orphans would wake up before the sun, have breakfast, and were then put into a clean room. We spent our mornings rocking back and forth.

Some children would get into fights and hit each other. Some would get into fights with themselves. Some would hit themselves so hard that the people in charge would dress them in a piece of cloth that tied their arms around their little bodies so they couldn't move. For those who kept being bad, the workers would force them to swallow little pills that made them go to sleep.

By lunchtime, everyone woke up, ate lunch, and did the same thing all over again until dinner. After dinner, we got cleaned up and put to bed. That's how life was. It was very orderly.

Many times, the people in charge were mean to us. Some of the smart kids would get together to try and stop the people in charge from hitting the other children. But it didn't work because the people in charge got meaner.

There wasn't any hope. I think that's what made some of the children hit themselves because they *really* wanted to hit the people in charge, but they weren't big enough to make that happen.

No one ever told me about Jesus.

One night when I was asleep, a very nice man with peace on His face came to me in a dream. He told me that everything was going to be all right, and whenever I was lonely and scared, I could talk to Him, inside my head, quietly, so no one would know. He said that He would hear me, though, and He would listen.

This man with peace on his face told me that His name was Jesus and that He suffered too. He told me that the people in charge beat him and tied His arms up so good that He couldn't move them either.

And while He was hanging there on a cross, He asked His Father in heaven to forgive all the people who were mean to Him, and then He died. But He did it all for us because He loved us so very much.

After this dream, I had a peaceful feeling that everything was going to be all right.

Then one day, something happened to the people who were in charge of our entire country. Nicer people took over, and we started getting visitors who wrote stories about the orphanage where we lived. They took pictures and showed them to thousands of people all over the world. Then we got lots more visitors.

These visitors would walk into the crowded room where we were all rocking back and forth, point to a child who looked like he was growing, and the next thing you knew, that child would go missing.

I was confused.

My friend Thomas told me that these missing children were brought to another country called America, where they were killed. He said their body parts were sold for lots of money. I felt pretty lucky living in the orphanage because even though things were not safe, I got to keep all my body parts.

ORPHANAGE

Chapter 2

Adopted!

One day, two visitors who couldn't stop smiling came into the crowded room and pointed at me. I got a bath and clean clothes, and the people in charge told me I was going for a train ride and wouldn't be coming back. I thought I was going to be dragged to America, where I would have my legs cut off and sold to some rich person who didn't have any.

But when I thought of the man from my dream, when I thought of Jesus, I stopped worrying about being sawed in half.

These smiling people took me on a train with six other smiling people and three other children like me. The train carried us down the map to a place called Bucharest.

When we got off the train, I looked around and noticed that not one person was sitting on the ground, rocking back and forth. They were doing other things but not that.

My smiling people gave me crackers shaped like fish, and I ate them until they were all gone. Then they gave me a piece of bread, and I held onto it so tightly that the bread got squished flat and hard. I ate that too.

The grown-ups put on different clothes and took us children to this place where people sat around big tables and ate lots of food. We were rolled in strollers and parked beside the legs of the table. It's hard to believe, but there was so much food in the baskets that one piece of bread toppled out and onto the floor. Us four children jumped out of our strollers and fought over that roll, hitting each other as hard as it took.

It was looking good for me, but the adults pulled us apart and put us back in our strollers. Then we were each given a clean roll from the table. The dirty roll was thrown into the garbage. Do you believe that? I wanted to run and get it out, but sometimes you just have to let things go.

In the morning, my two smiling people told me what we were going to do next, but I had no idea what they were saying. I told them that I did not want any of my body parts taken from me. But they didn't understand anything that I said

ROMANIA

either. So we were even. They kept handing me food, so everything was okay…
so far.

We got into an airplane, which I never knew existed, and stayed in there
forever. I rocked back and forth. Whenever I stopped eating, my new parents
would hand me something else to eat. I thought they were taking me to heaven,
up above the clouds where Jesus' Father lived, where no one was ever hungry.
But they weren't. They were taking me to their house in America, where there
was a sign hanging on the front door that read, "Welcome, Andrew!"

After the celebration was over, they took down the sign, folded it, and put it in
a clean drawer that worked without shoving it. I thought maybe they would use
that sign again when this family adopted the next "Andrew," but that never
happened again. I still can't figure out why they kept that sign.

Chapter 3

New Dad, New Mom

My new dad talks a lot. He talks to people over the phone, he talks to people in his office, he talks to people at restaurants, and on Sunday mornings, he talks to an entire room full of people who listen very closely.

This is what he does for a living. He gets paid to talk. He talks all the time, except when he comes home. Then he's quiet. I would talk more, but no one understands what I say. Everyone understands my new dad but me.

When my new dad goes off to work, I stay at home with my new mom. She talks too, but no one's there. Well, I'm there, but I have no idea what she's saying. Sometimes she will be in a room all by herself and talk.

I have decided that talking is very important in America. I have decided that I'm going to have to learn to talk like Americans so people here understand what's going on inside my head. Maybe someday I'll have something important to say, and it is best to be ready for things like that.

One time my mom was in her closet trying on clothes that didn't fit, and she said to herself, "What in the world do we have here?" She tried to put on a pair of shoes, but her toes ran smack into a piece of bread that was hiding in there.

She yanked the bread out and threw it away. Do you believe that? I do not understand this throwing food in the garbage. I tried to explain to her that I put it in there for a reason, but she just smiled at me, then hugged me and kissed me.

Over the days, my new mom found lots of hiding food. But it was when she found the piece of bread shoved into the machine that shines movies onto the TV that she did something about it. She led me to a huge book on the shelf that had beautiful pictures. We turned to a section written by a man named Matthew.

I couldn't believe it! There was a picture of the same very nice man with peace on His face, who had visited me in a dream. I pointed to the picture and said, "Jesus." My mom's eyes opened very wide. She was surprised I knew Him. She had no idea that Jesus was the first person to ever be nice to me. He was nice to me even before she was. But I thought He was made up. I thought He only lived in my dreams. I didn't know He was real. I didn't know He had pictures

of Himself in books.

When Dad got home from his talking job, Mom ran to the front door and threw her arms around him like she hadn't seen him for a thousand years. She jumped up and down. She told him about the big book. She opened it again to the picture of the man and said to me, "Andrew, who is this?"

I said, "Jesus."

She looked at Dad, and his jaw dropped so far open that it almost hit the floor.

She said to me again, "Who is it?"

I said, "Jesus, Jesus, Jesus!" I liked to say His name out loud. No one gets mad at me here in my new home. They liked hearing His name said out loud. We held each others' hands and danced in a circle, laughing and saying, "Jesus," over and over again. Then they sang a song about how Jesus loves us because the big book tells us so. It was a very happy day.

When I got into bed that night, Mom and Dad pulled the clean sheets up to my chin. They showed me how to pray by putting my two hands together. Then they prayed out loud. I shook my head no and placed a finger over my lips for them to be quiet. But they nodded their heads yes, and they said super loud, using their outside voices, "NOW I LAY ME DOWN TO SLEEP, I PRAY THE LORD MY SOUL TO KEEP. IF I SHOULD DIE BEFORE I WAKE, I PRAY THE LORD MY SOUL TO TAKE. AMEN." ("Lord" is another one of Jesus' names. I learned He has a lot of names, and He answers to every single one of them.) It was amazing to be able to talk out loud to the very nice man with peace on His face who told me that everything was going to be okay. And Jesus was right. Things were looking hopeful.

My mom and dad turned off the light but left the door wide open because, as you can imagine, I was very afraid of the dark.

But here is the good news for me. I have on clean pajamas, my very own slippers beside my bed, a dresser that opens and closes without shoving it, and a brave mom and dad who smile at me, most of the time. I felt like my life was beginning to turn out all right. I closed my eyes and quickly fell asleep because I knew that I had a loaf of bread in my top drawer, hiding under my underwear.

Chapter 4

The World's Greatest Invention

It was around this time I started to feel like my body parts were going to stay mine. I was also learning words that other people knew, which made sharing what was going on inside of me a whole lot easier. But for some reason, I was still always hungry. And if I wasn't hungry, I was afraid I would get hungry soon, and I was worried when I did, there wouldn't be any food left for me.

It turns out that I wrote best with my left hand, so I used that one to do everything. They wouldn't let me use that hand in the orphanage. I have no idea why.

In my right hand, I held my food. If I didn't have food tightly squeezed in my right hand, I became afraid and freaked out. As long as food was in my right hand, I was completely okay with every single thing that was going on in my life.

This one particular morning, after Dad left to do his talking, Mom gave me a bagel to hold. A bagel is really good bread because it has a hole in the middle of it, which makes it easier to hold. It's also good because no matter how hard I hold it, it doesn't get any more squished than it already was.

I was playing with my red truck. It has a handle on the side. When you push down this handle, everything in the back of the truck dumps onto the floor. I loved playing with my truck. I would pile Dad's paper clips into the back and then dump them out.

The problem was, I couldn't push down the handle with only my left hand. I needed both hands—one to hold the truck and one to push down the handle. But my right hand was already doing something extremely important. It was holding my bagel.

As you can see, I had a real problem on my hands. I sat on the floor in the living room for a very long time, trying to figure this out, while my Mom cooked us breakfast.

My mom could set the table, crack the eggs into the pan, and flip them over with no problem at all. Because she could use both hands for everything, things were easier for her. I could not. I was very frustrated.

I became so frustrated that I stomped my feet on the ground and watched them kick beneath me. It was then that the idea came into my head. I slipped a shoelace out of my left shoe and skipped into the kitchen.

My mom flipped the hand towel over her shoulder and turned to find out what was going on with me this time. I held the shoelace up for her to see, then the bagel. She did nothing. I showed her the shoelace again, then the bagel again. A deep line formed between her two eyes. She was confused. I knew this expression of hers very well.

I took the shoelace and stuck one end of it through the hole of the bagel, then pulled it through. I motioned for her to hang the bagel around my neck and tie it behind me. She smiled a big smile, then took both ends of the shoelace and did as I had asked. Wow! This was the world's greatest invention of all time! From that moment on, I could use both of my hands for everything. I was becoming more and more like my parents every day.

I liked my bagel necklace. I wore it everywhere. I never took it off, not even when I slept. And I no longer needed to hide loaves of bread in my underwear drawer. As long as that bagel was around my neck, when I got hungry, I didn't become the crazy boy from Romania.

You see, the memories of being hungry had been so deeply scratched into my brain, they weren't ever coming out. The time had come for me to move on.

Now that I had my food traveling with me, I was free to go out into the world with much more confidence. My panic attacks were happening less and less. And when Sunday came, the day of the week when no one in the world worked but my dad, my parents took me to church along with them.

Chapter 5

Sunday School

The only reason I let them leave me in a closed room with other children was because Jesus' picture was hanging on the wall. I also noticed that the children were not wrapped in cloth with their arms tied around them. Their arms were free, and they were not rocking back and forth. They played with toys. They smiled and talked with each other. And all the while, Jesus smiled down on us. So, when my parents left, I was okay with staying.

The person in charge invited us to join her at the table. She had something to share from a book, and we were supposed to listen. I didn't understand everything, of course, but I understood enough. The pictures helped.

The teacher explained that when Jesus walked on the earth as a man, He was so well-liked that people would swarm around Him like He was a famous rock star. His friends were worried about Him. They felt it was their job to protect Him from overly excited people.

One day, a bunch of happy children rushed towards Jesus, and His friends thought the children were going to knock Him over, so they tried to hold them back. Jesus said to His friends, "No, no, no. Let the little children come to me. They're the ones who are going to get into heaven the easiest because they don't have a lot of suitcases to carry."

I guess the older you get, the more suitcases you have, and the next thing you know, you're using all your hands and feet to carry the suitcases, and you have no hands left over to wrap around Jesus.

At that moment, I felt pretty blessed. Pretty blessed indeed. I never owned a suitcase! Ever! When I left the orphanage, I had only one set of clean clothes, and I was wearing them. This teacher in this Sunday school class told me that Jesus didn't own anything either. All He had were the clothes that He wore, and I have to say, He looks pretty well-adjusted to me.

Chapter 6

My Dad's Office

Fresh bagels aren't cheap. My mom had to rotate the old ones out because they got hard. Rock hard. We knew they got rock hard because one time I bit into an old one, and half my tooth fell off. My mom and dad had a serious talk. They decided that half a tooth wasn't a big deal because these were only my first set of teeth. One day a brand new tooth would replace that broken one. So they weren't worried.

I knew nothing of this new tooth business because I never had it happen to me before. I had to trust that what they were telling me was true. It's hard to trust when you haven't had the experience for yourself. I guess that's why I have to wear this bagel around my neck. People can tell me it's okay now, that I don't have to worry about going hungry anymore, but it doesn't take away the deep

fear in my brain. I wear the bagel necklace because it reminds me that my growling stomach is not something I will have to live with for long.

This day was different from the others. Instead of staying home with Mom, Dad took me to work with him. I was placed in that same room with a couple of other children and a woman I did not know. But Jesus was still there, hanging on the wall.

She told us a story that was hard for me to believe. She said that one day when Jesus was walking around in the world, thousands and thousands of people were following Him because He was saying some important things about how we should live our lives. He was sharing with people that His Father, who lived in heaven, would be able to give them the very best life if they would only put their trust in Him.

They were on a hillside and had been there for a long time, so the people were getting hungry because they were away from home where there was always food. There was no food anywhere on this hillside. The people were about to leave and run home because they couldn't take it anymore. The hunger pains were too much for them to bear. Suddenly, this little boy, like me, walks up to Jesus and gives Him his lunch.

Jesus opens the sack, and inside were five barley bagels and two fish. I don't know what got into that boy, giving away his food like that. I guess he trusted Jesus, or he wouldn't have been able to do it.

Thousands of people sat down in the prickly grass, and Jesus took those bagels and fish and lifted them up into the sky, thanking God for the little boy and his kind gift. Jesus then asked his disciples to hand out the food to the starving people, and suddenly, out of nowhere, there was all this food.

There was more to eat than anyone in their right minds could ever imagine. And every single person who was there ate till they were full. Thousands and thousands of people were so stuffed they all had to lie down and take a long nap.

Then Jesus gave the little boy 12 baskets of bagels and fish for him to take home to his mom and dad.

What was amazing to me is how that boy, who was like me, could give away his lunch, not knowing the end of the story. He didn't know anything about how God could take that little lunch and turn it into a ton of meals. I tried, but I could not get this story out of my head.

Chapter 7

The Crazy Boy from Romania

When nap time came, the new teacher said we all had to lie down on these mats. When I did, she tried to take off my bagel necklace. She said I would sleep better without it, but I said, "No." She wouldn't give up. She didn't know about the sleeping giant in me that turned into the crazy boy from Romania.

Without my permission, she untied the shoelace from behind my head, and I went nuts. I kicked and screamed till my shoes fell off. She tried to calm me down, but it was too late. Nothing worked, not even the picture of Jesus, who was still smiling down on me, even though I was behaving badly.

I yelled for my father, and they quickly brought me to his office, where all the talking takes place. They opened the door, and I ran to my dad. He embraced me, and after I felt safe, I calmed down.

I handed my dad the shoelace and the bagel that had taken a beating from me rolling around on the floor. And he tied the shoelace around my neck.

He was with a large man who had a red nose that looked like a warty pumpkin. This large man sat there looking at my dad and me, but said nothing. He was dressed in a suit with a tie and had a sack lunch with him, just like the little boy in the story with Jesus. My dad explained to the man that I was very attached to my necklace and did not want to be without it. The man reached behind him and undid a chain that had been hanging around his neck. He motioned for me to come to him.

I looked at my dad, and my dad nodded to me, so I thought it would be okay. I went to the stranger, and he told me that when you love Jesus with all your heart, you don't have to worry about being hungry anymore. He said that Jesus takes care of all that and more.

He opened his hand and in it was a cross hanging on a chain. He asked me if I knew what that was and I said, "Yes. That is where the people in charge tied Jesus when they were done using him all up, and wanted him to die."

The man said, "When Jesus died on the cross, He died for everything we are afraid of. In fact, he died for your fear of not having enough to eat, so you don't have to be afraid of that anymore."

Then the man draped the cross around my neck and latched it behind me. He said, "Now that you know this about Jesus, one day you might not have to tie this bagel necklace around your neck." I smiled at him, thinking that he was completely out of his mind. He did not understand my history of when I had *no food at all*. If he did, he would not be talking such craziness.

I walked back to my dad and took hold of his hand. I listened while the two grown-ups finished their talk. My dad asked the man, "So, how long has it has it been now, Charlie?" And the man said, "90 days, Pastor. I've gone 90 days without a single drink."

I thought to myself, *Geez, if this man with the red nose can go 90 days without anything to drink, maybe I could give up wearing my bagel necklace.*

Chapter 8

That Special Saturday

Talking seems easy for my dad, especially when he talks about Jesus. He spends a lot of time with Jesus, so I guess he knows a lot about Him. When people ask my dad questions or come to him for help, he knows just what to say.

But when it comes time for him to write down what he plans to say on Sunday morning, well, that's a whole other matter. On these days, on the days he has to write his sermon, he stays home.

He sits on the porch, arranges his pen and paper just so, and then stares up into the sky. If no words make it onto the page, he changes how he's sitting and then stares at the grass.

If that doesn't work, he leaves his pen and paper on the desk, lies in the hammock, and closes his eyes. And if that doesn't work, he packs up his things and leaves the house.

I never knew where my dad went. He would just disappear and say he'll be back when he's finished writing, or when the cows come home, whichever comes first. It was all a great mystery to me until that special Saturday.

My mom wasn't able to be home with me, so when my dad tossed his pen and paper into the garbage and headed out the door, he took me with him.

We drove, but not to his office at church, and not to see cows. We went to an awesome place—a place my dad says is very *holy*—the local donut shop.

My dad likes donuts, but he *really* likes coffee. The donut shop has lots of both. They also have the most amazing bagel-shaped desserts ever. And anything shaped like my bagel necklace is okay with me!

My dad ordered for us, and we sat down. He let me taste his coffee, and I spit it out because it tasted like dirt. He ordered hot chocolate for me. Yum, yum! He got out his pen and paper, then we waited for people to interrupt us. When I go out with my dad, the interruptions are the best part, and there are lots of interruptions. My dad knows thousands of people. And there are people he doesn't know, but they know him. My mom says that being out with my dad is like being at Grand Central Station.

LOVE THEM DONUTS
COFFEE Too......

My dad says he gets his best, most important work done at the donut shop, but I didn't see him write a single word. So I didn't quite understand what he meant by this until that special Saturday I will never forget.

Chapter 9

The Mission Field

We sat at a table like the others who weren't taking their food back to their cars. We sat there, and no writing was getting done. But we were enjoying our chocolate cream-filled desserts that we told Mom would be our *healthy* breakfast.

"Dad, you're not writing."

"Well, son, I don't really come here to write."

"Why do you come here?"

"I come here to make friends and introduce them to Jesus."

"Oh, so Jesus doesn't meet everyone in their dreams while they're sleeping?"

"No, not everyone. Sometimes He needs *us* to introduce Him."

As we ate and drank our hot drinks, a man who was not dressed in clean clothes walked up to the glass door and looked inside. He then pulled out a newspaper, placed it carefully on the cold ground, and sat on it. When people walked by him to enter the shop, he would talk to them, and they would hand him something.

I asked my dad, "What are they handing that man?"

"Well, Andrew. I think he's without a home, so he's asking people for money so he can buy something to eat."

"But he's not coming in and buying anything," I said. "Why don't we buy him something to eat?"

"Well, we could. I have an envelope here with our money for the week. If you'd like, I could ask the man what he would like to eat."

"Okay. Let's do that," I said.

My dad approached the man, and through the glass, I could see them talking. He then came in, ordered something, then brought it to the man. The man took the food and gobbled it up. My dad returned to our table.

"That was an excellent idea, Andrew. The man said, 'Thank you.'"

"He sure was hungry."

"I'm sure he was."

"Dad?"

"Yes."

"What's he going to eat later, when we're not here?" I asked.

"I don't know."

"He has no money and no home where there is always plenty of food. What's he going to do later when his stomach is growling, and no one is here to help him?"

"I'm not sure, Andrew. I guess he's grown used to being hungry."

"Like me. Like I *used* to be."

"That's right, but now you have a nice place to live, where there will always be plenty of food," my dad reassured me.

"But what is *he* going to do later, Dad? He's going to get hungry again. I know he is. He's going to get very hungry, and there will be nothing for him to eat!" I was so concerned about the man without a home that I did not notice the tears rolling down my cheeks. "What does Jesus say about people like that, Dad? What does Jesus say about the poor?"

"He says they will always be with us."

"There must be a reason for that. Jesus must have a reason to keep the

hungry around us, where we can see them regularly."

"I'm sure He does, Andrew."

I looked down at the bagel necklace hanging around my neck. I thought about all the comfort it had given me, but now I have this other necklace. And this other necklace reminds me of Jesus, who died on the cross and forgave everyone for being mean. And now, because Jesus is around, I don't have to worry about where my next bagel is coming from. Jesus does all that worrying for me because He loves me very much.

"I'll be right back," I told my dad. I walked outside and asked the homeless man straight out, "Do you know Jesus?"

He shook his head no.

"Okay. Then you are going to need this." I took my bagel necklace off from around my neck and handed it to him. "Now, no matter what happens, you'll always know you've got something to eat, close by."

I turned around, and there was my dad standing behind me. He took my hand, and we walked back inside the donut shop.

"You know Andrew, one day we'll go back to that orphanage where your mom and I found you, and you can share that message with all those young children there. What do you think about that?"

"I think that's a good idea," I said. "Dad?"

"Yes?"

"I want to thank you for coming for me at the orphanage, and choosing me to adopt, just like Jesus did."

You're welcome. And thank *you*, Son."

"For what?"

"For writing my sermon for me."

"You're welcome, Dad. Anytime."

That is how the world was turned upside down for me, when Jesus came to live inside my rib cage. I am not afraid of being hungry anymore, so I can spend all my time helping to feed other people who still are.

Before we left on our trip, Mom and Dad surprised me with a brand new backpack. Nice, huh? I have *three* sets of clothes in there. *Three!!!*

And Dad and I got on a plane, which was no big deal now, and we flew all the way back to Bucharest, Romania. Then we got on that same old train and took it north to the orphanage where my parents found me. And I shared bagel necklaces with all those frightened children who did not know Jesus.

I explained to them what it was like to no longer be afraid. And because I was wearing my new backpack, both my arms were free to hug each and every one of them.

THE END

ABOUT CLIMBING ANGEL PUBLISHING

Climbing Angel Publishing exists for the purpose of sharing stories of hope and encouragement, aiding in the gathering together of community, and supporting the process of betterment. The following books are available at ClimbingAngel.com and major bookstores.

<u>ADULT BOOKS:</u> *(Romans 8:28-30)*

In His Image, Sam Polson (English, Romanian, & Mandarin)
By Faith, Sam Polson (English & Romanian)
My Birthday Gift to Jesus, Lisa Soland
Without Ceasing, Dr. Dennis Davidson
SonLight: Daily Light from the Pages of God's Word, Sam Polson
Corona Victus: Conquering the Virus of Fear, Sam Polson
Art Bushing: His Diary, Letters, & Photographs of WWII, Art Bushing
Art & Dotty: His Diary, Their Letters & Photographs of WWII, Art Bushing
Trimisul, Stan Johnson (available in Romanian only)
The Prism of Prayer, Sam Polson

<u>**CHILDREN'S BOOKS:**</u> *(Philippians 4:8)*

The Christmas Tree Angel, Lisa Soland
The Unmade Moose, Lisa Soland
Thump, Lisa Soland
Somebunny To Love, Lisa Soland (English & Mandarin)
The Truth about God's Rainbow, Lisa Soland
God's Promises, Lisa Soland
The Boy & The Bagel Necklace, Lisa Soland
God's Hands and Feet, Lisa Soland
I Like To Be Quiet, Joni Caldwell

MORE CHILDREN'S BOOKS FROM CLIMBING ANGEL...

The story of the rainbow is not just an ancient story restricted to the pages of God's Word. The presence of the rainbow is an ongoing, living example of God's faithfulness and grace toward His people whom He loves. This is the very reason we need tell this story, over and over again, especially to our children. All the promises of God are real. And while the events told in this book occurred over 4,000 years ago, the promises of God to His people stand firm today.

Get your copies today! Available at your leading online bookstores.

Both GOD'S PROMISES and THE TRUTH ABOUT GOD'S RAINBOW share the story of Noah, the Ark, and the covenant made between God and His people.

Pick up your copies today, and be part of the ongoing story of God's promises being fulfilled.

I LIKE TO BE QUIET
by Joni Caldwell

Do you have a quiet child in your family? **"I Like To Be Quiet"** is the perfect book for a light-hearted exploration into how that unique personality can be best loved.

Share this new children's picture book with all those young people you know who seek comfort in who they are.

SOMEBUNNY TO LOVE

"I was completely captivated by this beautiful story." – Sam Polson, Pastor of West Park Baptist Church, Tennessee

"Somebunny to Love is one of the best treatments of grief I have read." – Rev. Sharon Roddy Waters, Disciples of Christ minister, Virginia

"Somebunny To Love is absolutely wonderful...for both young and old!" – Mark Kirk, Pastor of Calvary Chapel Knoxville

"Masterfully written..."
– Jeff Gordon, author and film historian, Texas